THE CONQUER LIFE MINDSET

FOUR UNIVERSAL FUNDAMENTALS OF SUCCESS

EXPANDED EDITION

TREY & AUTUMN HOLLIS

Title: The Conquer Life Mindset: Four Universal Fundamentals of Success [Expanded Edition]

Authors: Trey & Autumn Hollis

Description: The Conquer Life Mindset is based upon the experience of Trey & Autumn Hollis. It is a mindset model that was developed by Trey & Autumn after having gone through years of tumultuous circumstances together. They eventually began overcoming those circumstances after changing their view on life, and fully pursuing their goals and dreams. The Conquer Life Mindset is the result of their changed perspective and it serves as a practical guide of application so others may benefit and implement this mindset for success into their own lives.

Keywords: Personal Development, Self-Improvement, Life Development, Goal Setting, Success.

Published by: HOLLIS ENTERPRISES & VENTURES, LLC. – Royal Palm Beach, Florida

Publishing website: www.ConquerLifeMindset.com

Book Editing: Erin Schaffer & Trey Hollis

Cover designed by: Trey Hollis

ISBN-10: 1523629932

ISBN-13: 978-1523629930

Dedication

The Conquer Life Mindset is dedicated to our children...
Kiana, Tahj, Xavier, and Jax...
who continue being the reason why we push forward,
and to provide them the blueprint for a drama free,
successful, secure, and happy life.

Table of Contents

Introduction i

I. **AWARENESS** 1

 Awareness Challenge 9

 Self-Awareness 11

 Self-Awareness Challenge 15

 Social Awareness 19

 Social Awareness Challenge 23

 Strategic Awareness 26

 Strategic Awareness Challenge 31

 Awareness Wrap-up 40

II. **COMMITMENT** 43

 Commitment Challenge 54

 Commitment Reflection 57

 Are you committed to you? 58

 Blamer Syndrome 59

 Check your commitments 62

III. **FOCUS**   65

    Blurry Vision   67

    Focus Challenge   72

    The Combination   74

IV.   **ACTION**   79

    Are you willing to risk it?   82

    Action Challenge   85

    Mapping your course   87

    We all have problems   89

    I don't know where to start.   91

    Action Challenge: Tools and Resources   92

    Action Finale: Conquer Life Success Tips   94

Overview   97

Conquer Life Reflection   99

About the Authors   105

Introduction

Welcome to the expanded edition of *The Conquer Life Mindset.* We decided to edit the original edition in order to offer this version for those who prefer to not have the adult language in the content and also to expand on a few points throughout the book. There have been small additions and changes here in the introduction and throughout the book itself; but overall, the content is the same as that in the *No Filter Edition.* So without further ado, let's go over the purpose of this book and get started.

When we got the idea of writing this book, we asked ourselves, "Why do people need this book?" The short answer was, this book adds to your arsenal to achieve success in life. It's a good thing to have a great and diverse "toolbox" that can help you to achieve the results that you're seeking in life, right? Of course it is.

However, the long answer to that question was that *The Conquer Life Mindset* isn't just another self-help-motivational-speaker-style type of book - it's an *experiential report* and workbook, giving you the opportunity to immediately take action in your personal development journey. The stories and experiences within this book exemplify the mindset that we have used to unlock levels of achievement in our own life together, which continually build our potential to reach those goals and destinations in life that we seek to reach. You're going to read through some of the "trials and tribulations" we've undergone through our life together for more than 20 years now; in that time span, we uncovered four fundamentals that we identify as the basis for the Conquer Life Mindset. These four fundamentals are the reason why people need this book. As you venture forward and learn about each of these fundamentals, you'll learn why each one of the four is so powerful and how [when combined] they can help elevate your efforts in your life pursuits.

To give some perspective to this concept of *Conquer Life,* think about this - if you watch the news or just have the slightest understanding of what's going on in the world, you'll see that life isn't just a simple "la-di-da walk in the park." Life can be brutal and can back you into that corner of depression and self-pity that many have found themselves in at one point or another. Life can take your hopes and dreams and turn them into regrets and nightmares. Life can be cruel and can grind you into the pavement and crush every single bit of willpower and drive out of you...if you let it. Life is a force - like when we're in a pool of water. The force of life presses against us from all directions and it will destroy us UNLESS we decide to act, push back, and overcome that unrelenting force. For example, if we don't have income to support ourselves, we can suffer and fall into deep poverty.

Another example - think of learning how to swim; you have three choices:

1. Do nothing…sink…and drown [**we get destroyed and life wins**]

2. Tread water…floating in one place…not advancing in any direction…just staying alive [**stalemate…just staying alive isn't living and life still wins**]

3. Miraculously learn a mean doggie-paddle and SWIM! Aim in a direction that takes you to a destination [**when we gain the confidence to overcome life's forces to reach different destinations, we win - we conquer life**]

The key of life is represented in the power of choice. We have this amazing power to choose how we approach life. We can swim toward the wrong destinations sometimes - and many of us have, present party included; however, we also have the choice to maintain an unbridled level of resilience that allows us to push toward the right and good destinations. In consistently moving toward the good, we distance ourselves from the wrong choices of the past.

We sincerely hope that you are encouraged by this book and all that you will learn, and that you embrace the potential that you have within you.

- *Trey & Autumn*

"…if you don't know where you stand in life and who you fully are, you won't be able to know where you're going."

TREY & AUTUMN

One: Awareness

"The ultimate value of life depends upon awareness
and the power of contemplation rather than upon mere survival."
ARISTOTLE

"Who are you, Trey?"

I grew up in a loving family, but we definitely had our dosage of dysfunction like many American families. Drugs, alcohol, emotional abuse, divorced parents, and all sorts of other screwed up circumstances and scenarios were played out during my childhood. On the upside, there were the family vacations, road trips, Christmas cards full of cash, and genuinely good memories that I still cherish to this day. But it was the turmoil of my childhood that left me in a state of confusion.

It took a great deal of my adult life to finally come to the realization that I never knew who I was. I never had an identity of my own. I grew up abiding by the strict rules of my parents. I grew up walking on eggshells, always trying to please everyone else, trying to be the good kid that got the good grades. I never got to do what I wanted to do – high school sports, go out with friends, etc. I definitely didn't live a "normal" American childhood. So when I left home, I struggled. I didn't struggle with fitting in and being social...I was good at blending in and being a sort of a social chameleon; I could become whatever my environment demanded of me. It's how I survived my childhood. My struggle was me learning to just be me...because I didn't know me. If you knew all the details, you'd probably wonder how in the world I managed to turn everything around and get back on the right track.

Before life got better for me, it got worse. In my journey for a self-identity, I made some great decisions and some pretty messed up decisions. I married my high school sweetheart, Autumn, in 1998 – that was a great decision. But, I also followed the path of drug use that plagued family members before me – that was one of those messed up decision. I chased that gritty street life that so many others never recover from. I threw away great opportunities of education in order to live the "thug life." In other words, I definitely needed to have my head examined.

Fast forward to December 23, 2005. I figured that I had eliminated any possibility of a successful life due to one of my biggest screw ups [which actually turned out to be one of the greatest experiences in my life – I'll explain later]. I was in the SHU of the Miami Federal Detention Center on a probation violation, and I was depressed, angry, and hurt. I felt stupid, ashamed, and just plain pitiful. I was blaming everyone else for my issues and circumstances. I blamed my parents, my grandparents, the lady who pointed the Secret Service in my direction, and anybody else I could lay blame on. Nothing was my fault...I was just a product of what *others* molded me to be. I seriously questioned how I could be at fault for my life being in shambles.

As I was sitting in that cell, fussing at God about my sorry excuse for a life [it was the greatest pity-party ever], I had one of those moments of crystal clear clarity. I remember muttering under my breath, "Way to go, God. Thanks a lot." And then the thought that changed my life just popped up like a subtle little whisper, "I didn't put you here...YOU put yourself here." From that moment on, I fully understood what personal responsibility was and how powerful it can be for us. It was in that freeing moment that I understood *I am in control of my life*, and I didn't need to continue searching for an identity of who I wanted to be. I realized that I just had to accept who I was and eliminate the negative habits out of my life – so that's exactly what I did. I thought about my situation for the next five months, until my release date on May 23, 2006. I thought about how this experience was the beginning of truly learning what *self-awareness* is. Don't get me wrong. I didn't magically have life figured out at that time, but the journey I was destined for was finally able to take a foothold.

When I got back home from my "court-mandated sabbatical," I was determined to make positive decisions for myself and my family. I went through a few jobs in the next year and a half, and in September of 2007, a family friend overheard me talking about getting back into college. She knew I was entrepreneurial-minded, and she pointed me in the direction of a non-traditional adult-oriented degree program at a local university in West Palm Beach, Florida. I jumped at that opportunity…it was a chance to fulfill the promise I made to myself back in 1995 after dropping out of college after only one semester. I immediately began the application process and started classes on October 11, 2007 [yes, I remember the exact date because it was yet another pivotal day in my life].

Lots of life-happenings have occurred between then and the time of this writing [2015]: Autumn and I had a few more children, we graduated with our master's degrees, we landed decent jobs at the university we attended, and we're steadily increasing in life and living comfortably. Nonetheless, we've had tough times over the years since those crazy days, but we've been able to effectively process the rough spots and navigate through them while learning the valuable lessons that came from those experiences. More importantly, we both grew into a great level of awareness – we identified *who we are, where we were,* and *where we wanted to go in life.* Gaining this great level of awareness has been the formative centerpiece of success and growth for Autumn and myself– and now we pass this knowledge on to you.

Go for a drive and Awareness is everywhere

Awareness is everywhere, and it's simply having the knowledge and understanding of various situations and circumstances. Beyond self-awareness, there are other degrees of awareness that make up the totality of awareness in our lives. Within the Conquer Life Mindset, there are three levels of awareness: *Self-Awareness, Social Awareness, and Strategic Awareness.*

Check your mirrors. Every single red-blooded 16-year-old kid in America who has taken their driver's license test has heard the phrase, "Check your mirrors." Why? Because driving requires an INTENSE amount of <u>all three awareness levels</u>. Drivers must be aware of what is behind and in front of their vehicle [social awareness], other cars on the road, road signs, and the weather [social awareness], the route to their destination [strategic awareness], the speed of their vehicle [self-awareness], the condition of their vehicle [self-awareness], and potential obstacles in the road [social and strategic awareness], just to name a few.

This example of driving reveals that you are already engaging in these states of awareness on a daily basis, but the majority of people don't take time to really think about it. For the most part, we're not even conscious of our own levels of awareness. This is why *Awareness* is the fundamental basis of the Conquer Life Mindset; the key is to carry the practice of awareness into all other areas of our lives.

Awareness Challenge

Based upon the *Driving* example and the conclusions you may have drawn regarding the three levels of awareness, write out one of your own experiences in which the three levels of awareness are present.

_____

_____

_____

_____

_____

_____

_____

_____

_____

_____

_____

_____

_____

_____

_____

_____

_____

_____

_____

_____

_____

_____

_____

_____

_____

Now it's time to move forward...into Self-Awareness...

Self-Awareness

There's a lot of academic research on the topic of self-awareness due to its relevance to emotional intelligence [Google Daniel Goleman's work or follow him on LinkedIn]. In order to develop a Conquer Life Mindset, self-awareness is the most important of the awareness levels and this mindset model. Self-awareness provides us the opportunity to grow and develop.

In the middle of the forest

Imagine waking up in a log cabin in the middle of some forest [some old "It's been abandoned for 20 years"-type cabin]. After you look around the cabin, you find a ration of supplies and food that would last approximately one week. You, then, spot a map with a note that was under the supplies. The note reads, "If you are reading this, then you are ready to begin your journey. On the map that has been provided, there is a plotted location – your mission is to simply figure out how to get there." At this point, you become aware that you're in a cabin in the middle of a forest with survival rations and a map with a location that you must get to. In this scenario, if you don't fully know where you are, then you won't be able to plan a route to get to that plotted location. It's the same in life: if you don't know where you stand in life and who you fully are, you won't be able to know where you're going. This is why self-awareness is extremely important – once we know who we are, we gain the understanding of our own skills, abilities, and overall potential to fully determine where we are in life and plan the routes to reach the plotted locations of our visions and dreams.

However, self-awareness is more than just a superficial knowledge of self – i.e., our personality types, personal preferences in food or fashion, our likes and dislikes, etc. What Autumn and I found out about self-awareness was that we had to get 100% real with our individual selves. We also had to exercise a manner of awareness [or reflection] regarding our relationship. We had to go deep within in order to face our fears, our insecurities, our pasts, and our failures. On the flipside, we also gained the opportunity to truly relish in our successes, strengths, and experiences. We were able to learn who we are and to take ownership for our lives in every way.

Through our formal education, we were able to learn how our lives have been impacted by our childhood. Through self-assessment, we learned why we think and act the way we do, and why we raise our children the way we do. We learned what our "hot buttons" are and how our reactions affect us. Most importantly, we learned what we wanted out of life itself. The fruitful knowledge of self-awareness all starts with getting real and being honest with ourselves – and **THIS REQUIRES GREAT COURAGE.**

The tool we use for self-assessment is one that's common to the business world: the **SWOT analysis.** Normally, businesses use this tool when they are preparing a strategic plan for their future direction. This tool is easily adapted to our lives, as well. Technically, we're preparing a strategic plan for our own futures, and it all begins with this self-assessment to achieve self-awareness. If you are unfamiliar with a SWOT analysis, it's a very simple process. SWOT stands for:

- **Strengths** *[skill, abilities, relationships, knowledge, etc.]*

- **Weaknesses** *[areas of improvement]*

- **Opportunities** *[goals, ways to leverage our strengths, ways to move weaknesses into strengths, ways to improve and increase our knowledge/understanding, tools to gain knowledge/understanding, identification of potential calculated risks]*

- **Threats** *[current & anticipated obstacles, lack of self-confidence, fears, toxic relationships, energy vampires, and other kinds of distractions]*

<u>At the end of this chapter you will have the opportunity to begin your own SWOT analysis.</u>

In addition to the SWOT analysis, we also maintain open loops of feedback with close co-workers and friends, and our mentors. It's important to know how we are perceived by others. The particular feedback we look for is what our perceived strengths and weaknesses are, areas of improvement, communication effectiveness, etc. Some feedback may match our own self-assessment, whereas other feedback may provide insight [and opportunity] to particular areas we may have overlooked in ourselves. The feedback you receive is a portion of the information about YOU that will help you increase your level of self-awareness.

Self-awareness is the foundational piece of developing the Conquer Life Mindset to integrate in your own life journey. If we don't know who we are, then we can never truly prepare a plan to navigate where we want to go in life. Whatever your goals or personal ambitions may be, you've got to really tap into your inner core and *reach an understanding of who you are* in order to begin your journey – and *you've got to OWN who you are*.

Self-Awareness Challenge

In order for you to benefit from this section, YOU MUST DIG DEEP WITHIN YOURSELF as you reflect and respond to the self-awareness challenges.

1. SWOT analysis – fill in the sections below regarding your *strengths, weaknesses, opportunities, and threats. [Use an additional blank sheet of paper, as needed.]*

Strengths *[skills, abilities, relationships, knowledge, etc.]*

_____

_____

_____

_____

_____

Weaknesses *[areas of improvement]*

_____

_____

_____

_____

_____

Opportunities *[goals, ways to leverage your strengths, ways to move weaknesses into strengths, ways to improve and increase our knowledge/understanding, tools to gain knowledge/understanding, identification of potential calculated risks]*

_____

_____

_____

_____

_____

Threats *[current & anticipated obstacles to your goals, lack of self-confidence, fears, toxic relationships, energy vampires, and other kinds of distractions]*

_____

_____

_____

_____

_____

Refer back to this SWOT analysis, perhaps monthly, and make adjustments as you develop. This process will help you monitor your progress.

2. Feedback Loops

Write in five names of people you trust to give you honest feedback on what they perceive are your strengths and weaknesses. Once you have identified those five people, you can then approach them [either through email or maybe face-to-face] and let them know that you would be honored if they could help you out with your Conquer Life journey by giving you that honest feedback. If they agree, then be direct and ask what they see as your strengths and weaknesses. Again, you must be willing to accept and own what may be some tough responses when it comes to the weaknesses category. It's okay to be nervous and maybe anxious, but once you get over the jitters you'll be glad that you have this new insight.

1. _____

2. _____

3. _____

4. _____

5. _____

If speaking with someone face-to-face, make sure you have a notebook with you to write down their responses.

3. Self-Awareness Affirmations Exercise

This exercise is to help build your confidence and conquer any fears you may have when facing your shortcomings, and it is relatively easy. After you've completed the SWOT analysis and feedback loop challenges, go over your own self-assessment and the feedback responses. Every day, identify one of each – one strength, one weakness, one opportunity for growth, and one threat/potential obstacle to your growth. At some point during your day, look at yourself square in the eyes in a mirror and, speaking out loud to yourself, say:

One of my strengths is _____

One of my weaknesses is _____

BUT...I will open my eyes to opportunities that will help me grow and develop.

I will not allow the threat of _____ to take me from my course and my journey.

Remember to refer to this section at least every other week in order to make adjustments and to remind yourself of your on-going progress.

Social Awareness

In self-awareness we searched within ourselves. In this social awareness section, we'll assess our personal and professional environments – those places where we live, work, and play. Social awareness is important because we are impacted by the world in which we live, one with profound effects on who we are as human citizens of this universe. Think of *social media* – social media is a great vehicle for social awareness. Through *Facebook, Twitter, LinkedIn, YouTube*, etc., we have the ability to be aware of what's going on in the world. As we gain deeper understanding of our local and global environments, we gain the power to effectively navigate through life and achieve our ambitions.

Our individual lives are made up of the relationships we have with others – our personal intimate relationships and our business/career relationships. Through experiences that Autumn and I have shared, we found that the best way to assess our environment is to <u>LISTEN and OBSERVE</u>. We have to listen to the speech of our friends, our co-workers, the messages of media, and even strangers with whom we cross paths. The world is full of wondrous cultures, and to learn about the concepts and ideas of others and their various cultures is a move toward global engagement. Global engagement leads to greater opportunity creation – and social awareness is the key. We have to pay attention to the world we live in.

Back to the forest

To begin building our social awareness, let's take a trip back to that rustic-looking log cabin in the middle of the forest. Our mission is to get to a specific plotted location on the map. The main problem with our mission is that we have no clue where we are on the map. We simply know that we are in a cabin in the middle of a forest with limited supplies and a map. The next course of action is to step outside of that cabin and explore...or simply listen and observe. When we step outside of ourselves, we can better listen to [and observe] the world around us in order to gather a more clear idea, or picture, of what's going on. In the middle of the forest, we can observe the sun to gain bearings, seek out landmarks that may be on the map, or listen for water and other signs to help us on our journey. This metaphor is exactly how we have to approach the world around us as individuals.

For example, Autumn and I have a goal of opening a barbecue restaurant. We've always been entrepreneurial, and the BBQ dream comes from our collective love of the culinary arts and my own family tradition of smoked barbecue. To get started, we can't just go buy into a turnkey restaurant location and start barbecuing, it doesn't work like that; instead, we have to take our time to research costs, locations, local demographics, menu development, local business regulations, health department guidelines, etc. From the research we conduct, we can move forward and develop a business plan. We'll need to create forecasts for budget figures, marketing, and all of the other facets of opening a restaurant. This is a prime example of social awareness: we educate ourselves on our surroundings with our goal in mind. This crosses over into whatever it is in life that you want to do. You'll need to gauge the requirements, obstacles/threats, personal and professional relationships, and your own abilities in relation to your goals and ambitions. Once we assess the various parts required to achieve our goals, then we can plot where we stand in relation to our goals. Once we assess our surroundings in the middle of that forest, then we can locate where we are on that map in relation to that plotted point that we need to reach.

Social Awareness Challenge

For this challenge, you must <u>choose one of your life goals that you are seriously committed to and would like to focus on</u>. Write your goal below and research what it will take to reach that goal. This is an in-depth challenge for you to really get acquainted with your goal and the landscape you will have to travel through to reach it. Be sure to refer to your self-assessment results from your SWOT analysis, and include those results in your findings.

Goal

_____

_____

Requirements to achieve your goal [write down your research]

Use extra sheets of paper, as needed.

_____

_____

_____

_____

_____

_____

Strategic Awareness

Have you ever taken a road trip? Do you remember how excited you were to hit the road and travel? Do you remember the road signs and billboards with advertisements of restaurants, tourist spots, or maybe even a theme park along the way? *That's the road of life.* We all travel this road, and we all have our destinations. On the road of life, those billboards are the various occurrences that happen in each of our lives. Some occurrences require our full attention – such as family issues, medical issues, or maybe financial reasons – while other occurrences are more like "temptations" that we allow ourselves to be distracted by and cause us to stray from the direction of our desired destination. No matter what happens in life, or what distractions we encounter, we all have the potential to reach our destinations, as long as we strengthen our strategic awareness.

Strategic awareness is likened to an internal GPS that builds upon increased self and social awareness. Within our strategic awareness ability, we form the vision for WHO and WHAT we want to become in this life. Strategic awareness is present in *everything* we do – career, parenting, physical fitness, recreation, etc. It becomes your plan to set out to achieve your goals and ambitions in life. There will be times when we must take time out to handle family matters or other intensive issues and uncontrollable circumstances that we all face in life. During those times, we must exercise our strategic awareness and be flexible in how we go about rerouting our course in life in order to maintain commitment toward, and focus on our goals. Simply put, never forget your goals, no matter what comes before you in life. Something pops up? Take the necessary time to grieve, or to handle the issues, and when things begin to level out…get right back on your route.

SQUIRRELS!

If you've seen the Pixar/Disney movie *Up,* then you may remember the "Squirrel!" scene. In this particular scene, a dog is "talking" to an older man when the dog's concentration is suddenly broken. He quickly looks in another direction, and yells, "Squirrel!", pauses for a second and returns to continue his conversation with the man. We all have those little "squirrels" in life that can pull us from our road long enough to make us forget our intended course. They can come in many forms and some are external, but many happen to be internal.

Sorting out relationships

Some relationships can be beneficial to our progress and some can be toxic to our progress. The beneficial relationships aren't an issue – these are the relationships in which our friends and family encourage us to pursue what we want without being offended that we don't have as much time to give them as we once may have. The toxic relationships are the ones that we have to diminish if we want achieve. The toxic folks are the ones who doubt us or make subtle attempts to discourage us from what we are seeking to accomplish. They can be *energy vacuums*, demanding of your time in order to pour their issues onto you or only calling when they need something. They typically do not respect your growth or progression toward an *improved you*. These are the people with whom you must exercise your right of "NO." Not in a rude manner, but in a way that kindly [yet firmly] sends the message that you are on a journey that requires your full attention. Toxic relationships require you to set boundaries in order to minimize distractions while you are en route to your destination in life. Who knows? Some of these people may become inspired by you and decide to embark on their own journey for the better.

You are your own worst squirrel

Despite the vastness of external distractions we are bombarded with daily, the biggest "squirrel" resides within us. These pesky squirrels present themselves as procrastination, poor time management, complacency, and – the big critter – self-doubt.   These are just a few ways in which we defeat ourselves.   We all have those moments of: "I'm not sure I can do this" [SQUIRREL!], or the "Ugh...I don't feel like doing this right now" [SQUIRREL!], and of course, the old "There's not enough time in the day" [SQUIRREL!]

In dealing with our own squirrels, Autumn and I have found that we have to be continually conscious of our focus and our decisions. We choose to do the things we *need* to do in order to be able to do the things we *want* to do. As such, we have been able to create a *happy balance* so that we may have recreational/vacation time, family time, and time to devote to our ambitions. There are a ton of various things that we could do now for immediate gratification – buy the 75" LED flat screen that we've had our eye on for some time, or buy those $150 Nikes, or even spend our weekends doing nothing productive.   Instead, we choose to sacrifice and focus our resources on achieving our ambitions; there will be plenty of time for those other things once we are where we want to be in life.   This is where self-awareness is crucial; once it is gained, we can identify our weaknesses [those distracting squirrels] and our own internal obstacles.

Strategic Wrap-Up...Squirrels in the Forest

You know the drill by now – back to the forest. With strategic awareness, we build upon our self-awareness and social awareness to fully develop a strategy to navigate the road of life towards our destination. We gain a deeper understanding of who we are and where we currently stand in relation to where we want to go. In the forest, after we've been able to pinpoint where we are on that map, we can then develop the route to get to that plotted location we were instructed to reach. We anticipate those squirrels along the way so we are not surprised, and keep a calm manner in being flexible and managing the issues that arise in our lives. Despite anticipated obstacles, through strategic awareness, we gain the confidence to conquer those obstacles.

Strategic Awareness Challenge

In this challenge, you will need to bring over that goal from the social awareness challenge. Write that same goal down, first.

Goal

_____

_____

Next, identify your squirrels currently prohibiting your journey to this goal [this may include some of the weaknesses/threats from your SWOT analysis, but go deeper and examine your relationships/friendships, self-defeating mindset, etc.]. Use extra sheets of paper, if needed.

External

_____

_____

_____

_____

_____

Internal

_____

_____

_____

_____

_____

Finally, write out how you would like to manage those "squirrels," both external and internal.

External

_____

_____

_____

_____

_____

_____

_____

_____

_____

_____

Internal

_____

_____

_____

_____

_____

_____

_____

_____

_____

Tough Questions

In this section, you will bring the wholeness of awareness together. The following questions will help you gather the *big picture* of how you perceive yourself and how you envision your future [and your purpose]. Refer back to all of your awareness challenges, as needed; again, dig deep to give yourself meaningful answers. Use extra sheets of paper, if needed.

How do you perceive yourself? Answer with your SWOT analysis in mind.

[Are you giving, selfish, empathetic to others, open-/close-minded, strong-willed, stubborn, passionate, careless, clumsy, etc.?]

_____

_____

_____

_____

_____

What do you desire from life?

Think of your goals and long-term vision. Write [describe] a vision of your future life at 10-, 15-, and 20-year intervals.

_____

_____

_____

_____

_____

_____

_____

_____

_____

_____

_____

_____

_____

_____

What is your WHY? [i.e., your purpose, motivation, or inspiration, etc.]

_____

_____

_____

_____

HOW do you plan on achieving the vision of your future?

This is the foundation of your *plan of action.*

_____

_____

_____

_____

_____

_____

_____

_____

_____

_____

_____

_____

_____

_____

HOW do you CURRENTLY react to adversities/obstacles?

_____

_____

_____

_____

HOW will you react to adversity/obstacles that attempt to sidetrack you from your vision?

_____

_____

_____

_____

_____

_____

_____

WHAT options for resources do you have to accomplish your vision?

Resources include people [relationships, mentors, advisors], skills, necessary tools [i.e., technology, cameras, computer, literature, education, etc.].

_____

_____

_____

_____

_____

_____

_____

_____

_____

What resources do you currently lack? How can you attain those resources?

_____

_____

_____

_____

_____

_____

_____

_____

_____

_____

_____

_____

_____

_____

_____

_____

_____

_____

_____

_____

_____

_____

_____

_____

_____

_____

_____

_____

_____

Awareness

Awareness wrap-up

Because we change as we mature and come into new information and ideas, we must always remain mindful of the impact that those various ideas and information have upon us. Awareness is an ongoing process, and it's okay to change and accept who you are and who you are growing to be. As you grow, you will notice that you begin raising your standards as to who you have friendships with, the places you go, and how you allow others to treat you. Accepting who and where you are in life right now provides you the opportunity to create a path to those plotted locations where you want to go...and the opportunity to get out of the middle of that forest.

You've now completed the toughest part of your Conquer Life journey. Getting real with ourselves is something that only the truly brave can do. When we were going through some of the toughest moments of our own personal life together, Autumn and I had to break down and figure everything out about ourselves and what we wanted in life. We have to continually face our weaknesses head on and make ongoing changes in order to reach the life that we strive to achieve. Once we were able to figure out where we were on that map, we were then able to create the plan to take us where we want to go...and we've been fully committed and focused to that plan since that time. We constantly stay aware of who we are and remain flexible in preparation for the *squir-rels* that sometimes call for our attention.

So keep going now…it's time to pick up momentum now.

"Are you committed?"

Two: Commitment

"Unless commitment is made, there are only promises and hopes...

but no plans."

PETER DRUCKER

Developing true Commitment

Remember those squirrels of distraction? They're always present, and may sometimes seem even more present when you are really trying to focus on your mission. Your commitment levels will continually be tested by them. But there's a cool thing about those tests: no matter the outcome, if we have the right perspective, we win. We win by opening ourselves up to learning from our missteps. Some people may get pissed off by their bad experiences, failures, or lack of awareness; others, however, will seek to learn from their experiences and make adjustments in order to improve their performance and results. The pissed-off folks are the easy quitters or mediocre-type people - they were never committed in the first place, their project was just a "good idea" [and we've all been there at one point or another]. The *truly committed* are the resilient ones who push through adversities and *squirrels* with persistence. They truly BELIEVE in achieving their goals. *Commitment = Belief.*

Question your motives

The key to commitment always leads back to the "Why?" that we individually set for ourselves. We have to constantly remember why we are setting out to accomplish that certain goal. For example, the "why?" for Autumn and myself with *Conquer Life* is to help people achieve success in their lives and accomplish their goals. We know how it is to go through extremely rough times in life, and we've been able to reflect and determine how we survived. With the life experience we've gained, we choose to pass on the knowledge and help others rise to the peaks of their own mountains in life. We know how it is to get turned down when we needed help, so we have developed a larger mission to create a non-profit that assists people through their circumstances. To meet our goals, we are driven by our desire to help others. This is our "Why?"

Your "Why?" is for you to determine. Don't think of your "Why?" in terms of its grandiosity, or lack thereof. Don't diminish your own "Why?" by thinking it's not good enough or grand enough. The reasons you have for your goals are YOURS. However, the one motive we warn against is MONEY! Don't fall for the motive of obtaining money. Doing something primarily for the purpose of money is one of the biggest traps of life...ever [sponsored by your wonderful friends at Unhappiness, Inc.]. There are countless people in the world that pursued their professions simply because they were drawn to the money; and within that bunch, there are a ton who absolutely hate what they do. Don't do anything strictly for the purpose of obtaining money.

When you're truly committed, you obsessively think about that project or mission or whatever it is that you want to accomplish on a daily basis. If you don't make progress on your mission, it gnaws at you – THAT'S OKAY! Don't feel bad when you get that gnawing feeling, it just means that you are serious about your mission and have a deep inner passion for it. Don't beat yourself up in those times, embrace that gnawing feeling and use it to further fuel your commitment and drive.

ZenSites Web Design... it was a "good idea"... kind of...

The short version of this story is that I spent 2014 building a business I wasn't really committed to. The full version provides an example of one of my moments of false commitment. Back when Autumn and I jumped into our first business, I knew we needed to start a website. I didn't know coding, so I looked for one of those easy DIY web design sites and I was committed to learning how to construct websites. In 2006, there weren't many great DIY web design sites; however, I was able to find a few decent ones and settled on the most user-friendly. I learned how to build a website in about three weeks. From there, I got better and better at being able to create sharp, simple, and clean websites. I never really thought about starting a website design business, but in 2014 that's exactly what I found myself doing.

Coming fresh out of grad school, I was working my 9-5 gig, and I started my web design business on the side for the purpose of helping other entrepreneurs have an online presence. I was originally motivated by the opportunities to flex my business consulting skills that I honed in grad school, and to help others succeed. But then the healthy profit margin of the web design business became a little too attractive to me. I soon began commanding higher fees. I was able to make a decent extra income, and then it happened. I realized that I didn't enjoy that business. My joy for website creation became a chore I completed in exchange for money. I became frustrated with clients not fulfilling their end of our collaborative agreement and the amount of time that web design demanded of me. It wasn't fun anymore. So, one day, I folded. I simply decided that the money just wasn't worth it. I wasn't truly committed to the website design business – it was just one of those "good ideas," at the time. It wasn't something I was passionate about. Instead, I had a *false commitment* toward the web design business that ultimately became a *squirrel*. I was distracted from what I am truly passionate about, which is helping others recognize their power to fully *conquer life*.

Throughout 2014, that gnawing feeling remained with me, screaming in my mind, "YOU'RE SUPPOSED TO BE BRINGING CONQUER LIFE TO EXISTENCE!!!" And the *squirrel* would speak to me softly, in a whisper, "One more website...it pays $2,000...they need your help." And every single time, I'd yield – and my passion was pushed into the corner, while I constructed the next client's website.

Around December 2014, I made an announcement on my business social network page that I would be ending the website design service on December 31st – and that was the end of that. It's actually good that I went through that experience; it helped me to gain further self-awareness and a deeper commitment to *Conquer Life*. From there, Autumn and I refocused on our commitment to bring *The Conquer Life Mindset* to the public in 2015. We committed to truly serve and inspire humankind. We committed to our passion...our mission...our purpose. In this refocused commitment, we were able to get the website launched in early 2015 and subsequently began developing the formal *Conquer Life* concept. You're now reading the fruits of that labor...this book. And since you're reading this book, that also means that <u>you are on your way to walking your own path of purpose, in full commitment</u>.

Big picture - Stepping stones

Understanding the concept of commitment is a matter of simplifying what commitment is. This perspective on commitment comes from the life experiences that Autumn and I have shared together since 1998. In the *Conquer Life* formula, there are two regions of commitment – the *big picture* and *stepping stones.* The *big picture* commitments are the specific large-scale things you'd like to do in this lifetime. Your *big pictures* are whatever you envision them to be, such as that beautiful home you've always wanted, or the awesome family vacations, or maybe starting a non-profit organization that grows to change the lives of millions, or writing that book you said you'd write one day, or opening that business you planned out, or getting that degree you said you'd get one day. These are the "big crazy fantasies" that we believe in for ourselves. These are the goals that make other people whisper behind our backs, "Pft...it'll never get done." These are the goals that make us say, "I don't know how I'm going to do it yet...but I'm going to do it." Develop your big picture because the "crazy" people have changed the world.

Our *stepping stones* are the small steps that lead us to our *big picture.* The steps that you take to keep good credit [so you can get that nice home or car], or maybe taking the steps to learn about business management and all of the particulars of entrepreneurship that you will need to know when you launch your startup or non-profit, or learning the process of writing a book and publishing it. Without following through on our *stepping stones*, we can never achieve our *big picture*. When we fully grasp the concept of commitment, we understand that there are no gray areas. True commitment entails uncompromising and resilient levels of focus [more about focus in the next section]. True commitment is an all or nothing decision that comes from within.

Beware of the "Good ideas"

Experience has taught me and Autumn that it's hard to be legitimately committed to someone else's "good idea" for you. Sometimes, those outside ideas come in the form of business opportunities that make an appeal to your emotional motivations. They'll tell you that you'll be able to "fire your boss" and "spend more time with your kids" and "take great vacations" – which all sounds great. The problem is that people jump from one of these opportunities to the next simply because they aren't committed to the opportunity itself – they're spinning their wheels chasing the _results_ they were sold on. Now don't get me wrong, there are certainly exceptions to the rule. There are some people who are given a "good idea" business opportunity and go on to hit a home run.

Those individuals are the true believers – they believe in what they are promoting, and they reap the rewards of that organic belief [or true commitment]. Nonetheless, avoid the trappings of "good ideas"; be aware of your motives and the "vehicle(s)" or *stepping stones* you are using to pursue your *big picture*.

If we aren't truly committed to the *big picture*, that lack of commitment will show up when we begin to take the necessary small steps, hopping the *stepping stones*. Procrastination and mediocrity settle in, and we don't really push to achieve. This happens when we amp ourselves up to chase a "good idea." When people put forth half-ass efforts, they get half-ass results and, then, quit because they didn't get the results they were wishing for. On the other hand, there is no mediocrity in full commitment. When we are passionately committed to something, we give 100%, never settling for the "good enough to pass" attitude. This is the attitude of a Conqueror – following through with maximum levels of commitment. If we get derailed or knocked down, we get right back up and back on track to push forward. Because again...*Commitment = Belief.* When we really believe in what we're striving for, we're not satisfied with settling or giving in. Conquerors believe they will achieve their dreams and are engaged in both their *big picture* and in the *stepping stones* to achievement of their goals, projects, and ambitions. Conquerors are committed.

Commitment

Commitment Challenge

In this challenge section, your mission is to write 3 of the *big-picture commitments* you currently have set for your life. Along with each *big picture commitment*, write out a brief list of a few of the *stepping stones* that you must take in order to reach the big commitment goals - [i.e., learning accounting, hiring, networking, getting a passport, saving money, learning about the book writing process, etc.]. Finally, gauge your true level of commitment for each of your *big picture* commitments using the scale given. The purpose of this challenge is to develop the habit of gauging your commitment level against the goals that you have set [becoming aware of what is involved to meet the *big picture*], and eliminating those that are simply "good ideas" rather than legitimate goals you are passionate about.

For this to be effective, <u>you must be honest with yourself.</u>

Top 3 Big-Picture Goals

Write your *top 3 big-picture goals* in the circles, and determine at least five of the necessary *stepping stones* in the spaces associated with each big commitment goal [use extra paper, if needed].

1.

What is your commitment level to this goal? [Circle the number that best applies]

1	2	3	4	5
Strictly for Money	It's a *Good* *Idea*	I'm Not Sure Yet	I Could Do This	I'm ALL IN!

2.

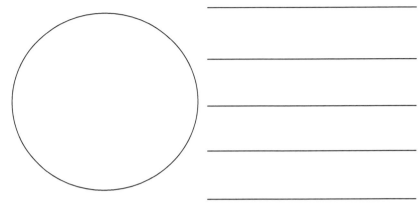

What is your commitment level to this goal? [Circle the number that best applies]

1	2	3	4	5
Strictly for Money	It's a *Good Idea*	I'm Not Sure Yet	I Could Do This	I'm ALL IN!

3.

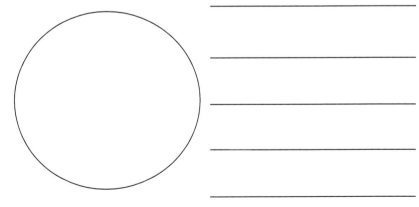

What is your commitment level to this goal? [Circle the number that best applies]

1	2	3	4	5
Strictly for Money	It's a *Good Idea*	I'm Not Sure Yet	I Could Do This	I'm ALL IN!

Reflection

If you were fully honest with yourself and think you may need to make some changes in your commitments, do so. You owe it to yourself to not waste any of your lifetime chasing "good ideas." I've spent years chasing after mirages of fulfillment, instead of buckling down and pursuing what I truly want in life. Don't waste time if you know better. If you don't have true passion fueling your direction, you're going the wrong way.

Are you committed to YOU?

Before you can truly be committed to your purpose and goals in life, you must first be committed to yourself. In my early teen years, I lived with my grandparents in Compton, California [yes, THAT Compton, California]. Both of them were educators in Los Angeles, and I attended junior high school at where my grandmother was a guidance counselor. The teachers and office administrators all had morning announcement duty on a "round robin" rotation system. There was a quote that my grandmother would always sign off with, "Remember...be good to yourself, you deserve it." That quote stuck with me. Now, it's a quote that Autumn and I cling to as we build our lives together. Even deeper is the true essence and meaning of that quote: in order for you to commit yourself to something, you have to see your high worth and value. You have to LOVE yourself and appreciate who YOU truly are. When you arrive at the point of increasing self-confidence, you will begin treating yourself like the beautiful being you are...inside and out. When you open up to self-acceptance [the good about you and your *works-in-progress*], you can commit to yourself. This self-commitment becomes unbridled, and you will not "sell yourself short" any longer. You will believe that you can accomplish what you set before you. You will have the fuel of Conquerors.

Don't develop the "Blamer Syndrome"

You see it and hear it every day in the news, social media, your workplace, your local community, politics, etc. - the blame fairy sprinkles blame dust on people's heads and lulls them into the *Blamer Syndrome*. The symptoms of this syndrome may include: denial, immaturity, irresponsibility, mood swings, name-calling, and bitterness toward others for our circumstances; however, there is a cure for *Blamer Syndrome*: a healthy ongoing dosage of *personal responsibility.*

When we arrive at that level of committing to ourselves, we must also OWN responsibility for our actions [or lack thereof]. <u>The journey of personal development demands personal accountability</u>. You can't blame others for your circumstances if you decide to "drop the ball" in life. For example, if you need to learn a new skill to prepare for a job you want, whose responsibility is it to go out and learn that skill? Whose responsibility is it to find out where you can take a class to learn that skill? Whose responsibility is it to study? We can't put the blame on our high school teachers or college professors for not teaching us everything. We have to take it upon ourselves to go out and be *self-directed* in learning what we need to know and do in order to accomplish what we desire.

On the other hand, when we make a mistake, no matter how large or small, we must also bear that responsibility. We must step beyond the fear of admitting a mistake and being corrected. Being corrected is not a bad thing...it is an opportunity to grow. We must shake the fear of feedback. Feedback is also an opportunity to grow. Why do you think companies conduct immense amounts of marketing research and focus groups? They're seeking feedback so that they may improve their product or service. Companies are continually refining how they take on personal responsibility for their business because they understand what it takes to grow. This is what personal responsibility is about – growth. When we own our actions *and* inactions, we open the door to personal growth and development, and we slam the door on the blame fairy.

The follow-through swing

Have you ever seen a baseball player at bat? Or maybe a golfer tee off? Have you ever gone bowling? In each one of these sports, and in others, there is the empowering process of the *follow-through*. The follow-through is the evidence of true commitment. The follow-through is where the power of your actions and planning are fully realized. The follow-through is when execution is put into play and you enter the last stage of full commitment. The follow-through is the "no turning back now" part. This is why it's important to fully gauge your commitment level to a project that you may be considering. If you come to realize you are not truly committed to something, DO NOT FOLLOW THROUGH...QUIT, and cut your losses. If you go forward without authentic commitment, you risk becoming miserable and unhappy with what you're doing, leading to bitterness, anger, and self-resentment. Follow through on those plans that you are truly passionate about; ditch the ones that are just "good ideas."

Check your commitments

There is no written challenge for this section. Instead, we pose summary questions for you to think about and address to yourself.

1. Are you fully committed to yourself? If not, what is preventing you from full self-commitment?

2. Are you able to look within yourself and be willing to own your actions and choices to obtain a greater level of personal responsibility?

3. Are you willing to follow through on your true commitments?

Commitment is a confusing issue simply due to our human nature. If we don't stay aware of our emotions and actions, we can get caught up in chasing anything the wind blows our way. To avoid being "wishy-washy, " we've got to value our time, efforts, and vision – this is where we will find the heart of our commitments. So, if you've decided what you truly wish to be committed to and are willing to accept responsibility for your life and follow through in your commitments...it's now time to get focused. Let's go on to the next section.

Three: Focus

"Your destiny is to fulfill those things upon which you focus most intently. So choose to keep your focus on that which is truly magnificent, beautiful, uplifting and joyful.
Your life is always moving toward something."

RALPH MARSTEN

Focus, Focus, Focus

Being a student of the personal and professional development industry, you are more than likely familiar with the buzz phrase, "Laser-like focus." And everything you've read and every video you've watched on the subject is pretty much right on point – in order to be successful in whatever endeavor you've set out to achieve, you've got to be fully focused on it. However, the issue of focus is more intricate than just a "laser-like" intent. Focus builds upon the second fundamental section of the Conquer Life Mindset, "Commitment." When you develop this mindset, focus is the bridge which carries your commitment to meet your vision. Without resilient focus, your commitment means nothing; these two portions work together as you strive to achieve your goals. Without full focus and commitment, your ambitions will fall into that "good idea" category. Now buckle up and get ready to go further into your new mindset.

Blurry Vision

As we've established, focus goes hand-in-hand with commitment. Without focus, you won't be able to stay true to your commitment, and you will allow those *squirrels* to invade. When the *squirrels* invade, you get pulled away from what it is that you want to accomplish – this results in you being <u>spread thin</u>. When people fall into being spread thin, they develop what we refer to as *blurry vision*. *Blurry vision* is when your focus becomes diminished and you lose sight of your *big picture* and even those *stepping stones* that move you toward your *big picture*.

Blurry vision is also spurred by a habit that we refer to as the *Superhero Syndrome*. *Superhero Syndrome* occurs when we try to be "hands on" in all aspects of our life and other people's lives, essentially trying to be a "savior" to others in any area that we can. How will you be able to work toward your own vision if you're always wrapped up in other peoples' issues? It's one thing to become a professional coach, mentor, psychologist, missionary, teacher, doctor, consultant, or any other professional that assists people with their issues. However, if you're not striving to be in any of those fields, and you're constantly being pulled into other people's drama, then you're simply a *rant mat*. And as a *rant mat*, <u>you burden yourself</u> with the role of a "Superhero" in order to try and solve the problems of others, which results in you neglecting to build a life for yourself. This also applies to taking part in others' projects when you have your own projects to consider and tend to. But when you're able to take the blinders off, own your life, and accept full responsibility for the purpose of your life and growth, then you take a great step toward true happiness and satisfaction.

Now, here's an exception. Sometimes, there are life events that we have to handle – whether it's a family issue, death of a friend/family member, sudden illness, or any other major pressing issue, those are the exceptions to breaking focus. Those are the life events in which you must give yourself time to work through those unexpected circumstances. The key to maintaining your focus through those types of life events is to temporarily store your commitment [*big picture*] in the corner of your brain that houses your "to-do" list. If what you're committed to is genuine, you won't lose focus of those *stepping stones* OR your *big picture*, and you'll be able to get right back on track after you've had time to handle and process those unavoidable life events.

Outside of those situational life events, there will be some things that you can control and others that you can't. Being able to discern between the controllable and uncontrollable is another key to achieving success and to fighting our own *Superhero Syndrome*. And, of course, when it comes to focus, never place focus on things that you have no control over. It's important to be aware of the uncontrollable situations but never place focus on them. Your focus must always be directed toward the things that you do have control over. Those things that you have control over are the areas where you can create change in your life and bring about solutions to controllable problems. This is how you combat *blurry vision* related to your future ambitions, goals, and ideas, and this is why focus is so important.

Dismiss the distractions

We've covered what distractions are [*Squirrels!*] Now we're going to zero in on how to dismiss distractions or how to deal with them if you can't dismiss them. Ultimately, we all have to make our own individual decisions on what is a distraction in our life and what isn't, but the general rule of thumb remains: if something pulls you away from your intended path and you develop a case of *blurry vision*, it's more than likely a distraction. We're attacking this topic again because it's extremely important that people fully understand the need to be aware of current distractions and of the potential ones, as well. This topic cannot be stressed enough. The distractions of life that come against us are the same for everyone; they come in the form of people, obstacles, negativity, bad habits, and much more. Your focus, however, <u>has to come from within.</u> You'll never be fully focused on YOUR future life when you are distracted by the naysayers, bad habits, and negative people that may exist in your current life.

If you really want to defeat distractions, you've got to have a personal [and written] mission statement, and the determination to depart from those people, places, things, and activities that don't align with this statement. Your mission statement must outline who you are and what you have decided to commit yourself to [refer back to the Awareness and Commitment sections if need be]. Review your personal mission statement at least once per week [daily is even better] until it fully becomes a part of your very essence, a second nature. When you are constantly mindful of your personal mission, there is no longer room for distractions. Your personal mission statement becomes the compass for your purpose; it becomes your heartbeat – the very thing that you are living for. And, more importantly, your focus and commitment will be driven by your personal mission statement. Where your true mission is, your subconscious actions will follow.

Focus Challenge - Death to Distractions

In the first challenge for *Focus,* you'll need to face your distractions. Whether they are people, places, bad habits, things, etc., you'll need to lay them all out [or at least as many as you can think of]. The purpose of this challenge is to become aware of what is keeping you from progressing in your desired direction.

Write your answers to the questions below.

Use additional blank sheets of paper, as needed.

1. Make a list of your current distractions. Remember to think about people, places, activities, bad-habits, or any other thing that diminishes your focus and produces *blurry vision* for you.

_____

_____

_____

_____

_____

_____

_____

_____

_____

2. Do you sometimes fall into the *Superhero Syndrome?* If yes, do you feel that your tendency to rescue others has pulled you away from your own journey? What actions will you take to reduce your distractions and/or the *Superhero Syndrome* tendency?

_____

_____

_____

_____

_____

_____

_____

_____

The Combination: Awareness, Commitment, and Focus

Before moving on to the final fundamental, it's time to begin bringing the components of the Mindset, thus far, together. The thing about this mindset system is that all four [I will get to the fourth one, momentarily] of the fundamentals work together to produce a frame of mind that is powerful and purposeful. You cannot exercise just one of the fundamentals and expect to produce maximum and sustaining results for your life. You cannot exercise just two or three of the fundamentals and expect results. You've got to develop ALL FOUR of these fundamentals in a consistent and ongoing manner to maximize the potential for your life. And while we haven't reached the fourth and final fundamental just yet, it's extremely important to recap the first three fundamentals before moving on.

We've examined the foundation of the mindset in the first three sections of *Awareness – Self, Social,* **and** *Strategic.* Without *Awareness,* you really won't make much ground in your own development. In the majority of development programs, whether they're personal, professional, or otherwise, the first level of instruction is typically designed for people to "know themselves." For example, in sales careers you have to actually know your product if you are to serve the best interests of your clients. If you're a teacher or professor, you have to know your material in order to effectively pass on the knowledge to your students. If you're a pilot, you have to know your plane in order to safely complete your travels. There are millions of other examples to stress the importance of self-awareness and the accompanying awareness categories, but ultimately, you've got to implement ongoing awareness in your own life to really embrace the enlightenment that you will gain. If you feel the need to go back to the *Awareness* section to really gain a deeper understanding, by all means do it for your own success and the success of others whom you'll interact with and influence on a daily basis.

Next, there's *Commitment.* Remember, without <u>true commitment</u> to the goal that you've set before you, you're just chasing a "good idea." You know how New Year's Day rolls around and all of a sudden people have all of these common resolutions? "Hey, I'm going to lose weight!" or, "I'm going to quit _____!" We've all made a few of those "good idea" resolutions, but by March, we realize that we never really intended to accomplish those goals. When it comes to those kinds of "good idea" resolutions in life, it turns out we are simply caught up in the excitement of the New Year or the thought of the *big picture* without ever contemplating the small steps we'll need to be committed to conquering in order to reach the *big picture*. <u>*Big Picture - Stepping Stones*</u> is the organic message of commitment – keep your *big picture* in mind, but make sure you never negate the *stepping stones* to reaching your final goal. Also remember, if you are pursuing a business or any other type of venture in which money is a reward...NEVER let money become your primary driving force. The moment you lose yourself to money is the moment you've sold out on your original purpose and/or goal.

Another part of commitment is being committed to yourself. In being committed to yourself, you'll develop a strong level of awareness, and you'll be able to navigate your life strategy with skill rather than just blindly jumping forward. You'll take on a high level of *personal responsibility* and set forth to learn other perspectives and knowledge to build your *mindset toolbox* for your journey [just as you are right now by reading through this book]. Those who live with high levels of *personal responsibility* NEVER welcome the blame fairy. *Personal responsibility* is what commitment rests in – accepting ownership of our lives and pushing forward to truly embrace the fullness of who we are and all that we can be.

And then there's the cousin of commitment – *Focus.* Remember the *SQUIRREL!* from the *Awareness* section? Those "squirrels" are central to all of the fundamentals of *The Conquer Life Mindset*. The enemies of focus, commitment, and awareness are those distractions that we allow to pull us off course.

YOU – AND ONLY YOU – HAVE THE POWER to push those distractions out of your way. Besides those particular life events over which we have no control, there is no reason why we should be inundated by toxic people or our own activities that will act as storms in our lives. Do not allow the fog of *blurry vision* to overtake you and infringe upon your own personal mission. Remember, your mission statement is a result of your awareness, commitment, and focus – PROTECT YOUR MISSION. In protecting your mission, you will be able to limit distractions and navigate where you need to focus your energy and time, doing so with pure intention.

And now it's time to move into the final fundamental.

Four: Action

"Successful people maintain a positive focus in life no matter what is going on around them. They stay focused on their past successes rather than their past failures, and on the next action steps they need to take to get them closer to the fulfillment of their goals rather than all the other distractions that life presents to them."

JACK CANFIELD

Who will stop you?

Guess what? You've got this immense energy propelling you now. This is it. This is the point where everything comes full circle. You've laid out a map for your future in the *Awareness* section...and you've assessed who you are and how you will navigate the path you've set before you. You're aware of the *Commitment* and *Focus* that your goals demand, and you're ready to take *Action* with integrity and passion toward reaching your goals.

So, who will stop you? The answer to that question is, you. Only you will stop you. By not taking the steps forward to achieve your goals, you kill any bit of momentum that you have gained to push forward. But if you realize what your distractions are and you anticipate what is before you, and you make conscious actions to overcome those distractions and obstacles, then you are serious about your mission. You've got to want it badly. You've got to be so determined that NOTHING will stop you from achieving what you want to complete. If you've ever seen the movie *The Shawshank Redemption,* then you know the story of the character, Andy Dufresne. He was innocent of the charges against him but was found guilty and subjected to a horrible experience in prison. But Andy didn't lose hope – he devised a plan of **action** to escape. His plan was to chip away at the rock wall in his cell and then finally escape out of the prison through a sewage tunnel - in under twenty years. He was determined...and he did not quit. And just like Andy, sometimes we have to go through a lot of low-points in order to reach our goals in life. Are you willing to endure the tough times to get to where you want to be? Andy was...and he gained his freedom by doing so. Andy didn't let anyone deter him from escaping the miserable prison that he was in...he took action.

Are you willing to risk it?

Taking action involves taking risks. You've always taken risks even if you don't realize it. Think about driving again...it's a risk every time you jump in the car and drive anywhere. You can't control other people on the road, but you have to do your best to drive defensively and anticipate other drivers' actions. Examining risk a little further, it becomes clear that stock investments, your retirement portfolio [do you know about Enron?], having children, starting a business, cooking, taking an airplane flight, eating at a restaurant, even walking down the street is a risk these days. These are all risks that many people don't really consciously consider. But here's the awesome thing about risk-taking: some are *calculated risks*, and others are *blind risks* – and you have a choice of the type of risks that you take. Calculated risks are wise and lead to calculated opportunities. On the other hand, blind risks lead to crushing defeats and demoralized self-confidence.

The biggest force that prohibits people from taking risks is *fear*. Fear can paralyze us and block us from taking action. Whether it is fear of failure, fear of looking like a imbecile to others, or any other kind of fear, we simply get hung up in our fears and never take the necessary actions to move toward realizing our envisioned life. However, when we engage in the three levels of awareness, we can, then, build that self-confidence to create our calculated opportunities and risks, and overcome the fears of stepping forward. The awareness section wasn't just for the sake of learning awareness – it's a foundation for creating your own calculated risks and opportunities. With ongoing practice in awareness, you'll develop a mind to think of various possibilities and to plan your route before just blindly jumping out there. When we develop our plans and increase our self-confidence, we realize we can take *calculated risks*. It's just like when start-up entrepreneurs develop a business plan – they make forecasts for marketing and budgeting, and they will devise back-up plans in case something doesn't necessarily go right. That's the perfect epitome of calculated risks. When we created this Conquer Life Mindset, we knew that our experiences could be used by others in helping to create their own opportunities for their lives, and taking action is the "glue" of this Mindset.

On the other hand, *blind risks* typically turn out to be setups for disaster and dream killers. Have you heard that old Ben Franklin quote, "If you fail to plan, you plan to fail"? Failing to plan is what blind risks amount to. When we choose to move forward on a risk, we are already stepping out in vulnerability, but if we don't plan our steps and fail in our attempt, some people just don't bounce back. After that failed attempt, some decide to play it safe from there on out because the pain was more than they are willing to bear again, and they go on through life missing all of the other opportunities presented to them in the future. This is where those who do create calculated risks have an advantage; with calculated risks, there may be some failure mixed into the equation, but there's also a lot of winning. People with a focused and committed attitude can walk through failure and gather a ton of knowledge on how to redo or reevaluate the approach to their plan the next time around, and they gain an arsenal of contacts and resources. But those who take blind risks just seem to get handed a megaton of failure without knowing where they might've gone wrong. Don't take blind risks; instead, learn the art of crafting calculated risks.

Action Challenge | Assess Your Risks

Write your answers to the questions below.

Use additional blank sheets of paper, as needed.

1. What are three projects in your past that you took *blind risks* going into?

_____

_____

_____

2. How can you turn those projects into *calculated risks?*

Project #1_____

_____

_____

_____

Project #2_____

_____

_____

_____

Project #3_____

_____

_____

_____

_____

Mapping your course and paving your road

When we set forth to develop an idea [whether it be a business start-up, hobby, or whatever it is that we want to achieve], and we actively plan and create those calculated risks, there is a very important aspect we must be mindful of: THINGS CHANGE. We can't see every single event before us, nor can we plan for every possible pitfall. So when we do begin planning, we must always be willing to adapt and change our plans, similar to how a GPS system will reroute the course if we miss a turn or there's traffic [obstacles] before us.

Another major point in mapping our course is being able to learn what needs to be done in order to do what we want to do. For example, there's a lady who wants to get into gardening in order to grow her own fruits and vegetables for her family, but she has no idea where to start [we'll briefly address the "I don't know where to start" complex toward the end of this section]. In this case, she would need to research home gardening and how to set up a garden for fruits and veggies. Based upon the information and knowledge she finds, she could, then, begin to develop a plan that would best suit her needs. This example goes for ANYTHING that we desire to achieve – research your topic, goal, or project, and then develop a plan to achieve it. Once you develop the plan, put the plan into action. There are other bits and pieces to implementing a plan, but this is the *big picture* to get started.

Uncertainty, ambiguity, and confusion

Sometimes we hit a "wall of confusion" in life. We may feel as if we just don't know what to do next. What direction do we take? Who do we consult with? What's our next move? Don't worry…it happens to everyone.

Things change. People change. Ideas change. Circumstances change. And we have to be willing to change along with everything else. In a quote illustrating this adaptability, Bruce Lee talked about being like water:

"You must be shapeless, formless, like water. When you pour water in a cup, it becomes the cup. When you pour water in a bottle, it becomes the bottle. When you pour water in a teapot, it becomes the teapot. Water can drip and it can crash. Become like water my friend."

Bruce Lee knew the importance of adapting to our settings and flowing with change. When we reach those moments in which we face problems that demand change, we must embrace them as precious moments. They are precious moments because they put us to the fire, and we can either be consumed by our problems and allow our momentum to be turned to ash, or we can use that fire to propel us to seek solutions to the problems. This is that point where you have to adapt and adjust to the changes that come before you – to become water. You've got to be willing to change your gears and redirect your route. Yes, there's a bit of repetition here, but for a purpose. This is probably one of the most important lessons Autumn and I have learned, and that is to embrace ambiguity. We've got to cope with uncertainty and make a decision to NOT be dismayed by those times of cluelessness. Running off of the momentum of the actions you've been taking to get to where you are will be enough to carry you through the moments of uncertainty, as long as you stay aware, committed, and focused on your goals.

We all have problems

Everyone faces problems and issues in life. However, not everyone has the fortitude to power through and actively [and aggressively] seek solutions. For example, look on social media and check out personal story articles floating around the internet; people have a tendency to complain and whine about their problems. And oftentimes, they wallow in the misery that they create by giving their problems power over their lives. Here's an even more absurd aspect about those who focus on their *pity party*: if you don't join in with them and whine about the problem, but give possible solutions for their problems, you become a "blame target." They'll say that you don't understand the problem, and they will make any and all possible excuses why your solution won't work for them. By the way, if you have these kinds of people in your life, put some distance between yourself and them, as they can potentially drag you down. They are the kind of people who notice everything wrong in their own life [and in the world] but have no desire to make changes to improve their life or circumstances.

But you? You're developing your Conquer Life Mindset. This mindset is about solving problems and overcoming struggles in order to live happily. When you operate by this mindset, you take action toward fulfilling your goals, ideas, and dreams. When we begin to conquer life, we embrace who we are at our core, and it is then that we truly begin to enjoy life.

"I don't know where to start"

"I don't know where to start" is one of the most common excuses that people make. The better statement would be, "I've got to learn where I need to start." Saying you don't know where to start is being problem-oriented; whereas, <u>saying that you are going to learn where to start is solution-minded</u>. Learning what you need to do in order to get started on something, whether it is to achieve a goal or initiate a project, is the first course of action; learning what tools and resources you will need brings you one step closer to achieving whatever it is you want. This point can never be stressed enough. Stop thinking you don't know how to do something; instead, focus on learning how to do it.

Action Challenge | Tools & Resources

Fill in the areas below, accordingly. Use additional blank sheets of paper, as needed.

List a project or goal that you want to achieve	List tools, resources, and knowledge that you **currently have** to use toward your project and/or goal	List tools, resources, or knowledge that you **need to obtain in order** to achieve your project and/or goal
(continued)		

Now use this table as a starting point to begin acquiring the tools and resources you need to further your efforts in your projects and goals.

You can no longer use the "I don't know where to start" excuse.

Action Finale | Conquer Life Success Tips

Here are some tips that you definitely will need to put into action as you move forward.

1. Get a coach or mentor: Guess what? Most great CEOs have a personal coach or mentor. Even Bill Gates has a coach. Those CEOs realize that a coach can help them to see perspectives they may not have noticed on their own. Those CEOs also recognize the importance of accountability and guidance in their decision-making process – personal and professional. It's always wise to have wise counsel.

2. Maintain positive thinking: Positive thinking isn't a joke. It doesn't mean that you have your head in the clouds with unrealistic expectations of life. No, it means that you maintain an optimistic outlook on achieving your goals and ambitions. Daily motivation is a necessity to keep pushing your mind in the right direction for your life. There are plenty of motivational videos on YouTube and other sites around the internet – use them daily.

3. Build a true support network: As I mentioned earlier, if you have people you interact with who are in a continuous state of negativity, you'll need to distance yourself from them. Seek new relationships with people who are supportive of your efforts and are of the same optimistic mindset as you. Also, seek a new network of those who are willing to assist you when and however they may, whether with contacts, resources, knowledge, or any other tools that may help to propel you in the direction you are seeking to go.

The Conquer Life Mindset: A Synopsis

This entire book was predicated upon the personal life experiences of Autumn and myself. We have trudged through some tough points in life, and we've celebrated some great triumphs. These days, we celebrate more and trudge less. We fully engage this mindset in all facets of our life. We move within our passions, and we do what we need to do in order to live how we desire. Are we multi-millionaire CEOs? No, we aren't. We're people like you, who have these amazing dreams for our lives. We're people like you, who want to leave a legacy for our family. We're people like you, who know that there is more to life than the daily commute to a 9-to-5 job, where we spend more time than with our family and end up with a multitude of regrets when we enter into the "golden years." Because of this Conquer Life Mindset that we've developed, we experience massive happiness and achievements in our lives, as individuals and together – and you can, too. You just have to dig in and make the decision to implement these four fundamentals into your own life with no more excuses or self-defeating talk. YOU have the power to truly achieve what you want. Other people are taking the reins and are gaining control over their lives…why not you?

Conquer Life Reflection

To close out, here's a breakdown of the Mindset. Refer to this when you feel like you're losing traction or you need to regain the Conquer Life perspective to get yourself back on track toward a better you and a better future for you and yours.

1. Awareness

a. Self-Awareness: Know who you are, know what your strengths and weaknesses are, know your opportunities, and know the "threats" that can deter you from your goals and purpose. Truly get to know yourself at your very core.

b. Social Awareness: Assess your surroundings – physically and professionally. Know where you are in life – your current job or career. Know the landscape of opportunity where you currently live [if you feel like you need to move to a new geographic location for greater opportunity, consider that move]. Know who your current network of friends and associates are. Know what your current resources are.

c. Strategic Awareness: Know where you'd like to go in life [if you don't know, that's okay – work toward those things that you are passionate about].

Know and/or anticipate the obstacles that may come before you as you embark on your journey toward your goals. Develop the strategic plan you will need to navigate toward your goals and ambitions.

2. Commitment

a. *Big Picture*: True commitments are those big picture scenarios that will pull you to where you need to go if you listen to yourself and your passion. Follow your true commitments.

b. *Stepping Stones* are those small "checkpoint" goals that lead you to the big picture as long as you are following your planned path.

c. *"Good ideas"* will lead you astray from your true commitments. Those "good ideas" are mere distractions [SQUIRRELS!] that will divert your attention from the path that you have set before you. Beware of the SQUIRRELS! of life.

3. Focus

a. *Focus* is the cousin of *Commitment,* and it works hand-in-hand with commitment. While commitment is centered on the overall achievement of your goals and ambitions, focus is what drives you to continually live out your commitment.

b. *Blurry vision* is a sign that you are losing sight of your overall commitment and that your focus is failing. Focus demands that you put your distractions to rest. Be aware of your distractions and make strides to dismiss them so that you do not develop *blurry vision.*

4. Action

a. **Calculated risks vs. Blind risks:** "If you fail to plan, then you plan to fail." – Benjamin Franklin. Don't just blindly jump into projects; do your research and due diligence in order to develop a plan of action. Taking calculated risks is a sign of success. Blind risks are a setup for failure.

b. **Map your plan – be open to change:** Although you'll develop a plan to achieve your goals, make sure that you are willing to embrace the moments of uncertainty. You must be open to changing and adapting your plan because, in life…THINGS CHANGE. "Be like water, my friend" – Bruce Lee.

c. Be bigger than your problems: We all have problems. Don't let your problems become your excuses. Be aware of problems, but always be solution-minded.

d. "I don't know where to start" is the great common excuse. Change your thinking to, "I'm going to learn what I need to in order to get started." Again, be solution-minded.

e. Tools and resources: When you learn what you need to do to get started, then you will know what tools and resources you'll need. Resources may include people and connections. Tools may include actual tools, like a video camera or a computer, or they will be what you need for learning [i.e., books, video instruction, etc.]

f. Coach/Mentor, Positivity, Support system: Get a coach or mentor for guidance and accountability. Stay positive and optimistic, and also distance yourself from negative or critical people. Build a support system/network of those who will cheer you on and help you in your efforts when and where they can.

And that's it. That's "The Conquer Life Mindset." You've now got what you need to have the mindset to conquer any and all obstacles before you. The only person who can stop you…is you. Make a commitment to yourself that you will not give up on your true dreams and goals in life. There are people who want to see you fail, and there are people who want to see you win. Be with the people who want you to win. We definitely want you to win…that's why we wrote this book.

Here's to the Conquerors.

#ConquerLife

About the Authors

Trey & Autumn and family | Graduation 12.13.2013

Trey & Autumn Hollis have been married since 1998. As a husband and wife team, they have been through some very trying circumstances in life. Despite those circumstances, they have continually excelled in their professional and personal endeavors. Trey and Autumn both attained Master of Science degrees in Leadership from the MacArthur School of Leadership at Palm Beach Atlantic University.

Being residents of South Florida, the Hollis family enjoys trips to the Florida Keys, and of course Disney World in Orlando, Florida.

They also describe themselves as "hardcore foodies" with a penchant for the culinary arts. Trey is a BBQ fanatic, who credits his BBQ smoking skills and inspiration to his father, grandfather, and great-grandfather. Autumn is a self-taught culinary artist who enjoys diverse international cuisines and cultural fusions.

Beyond their love for personal development and mentoring/coaching others, Trey and Autumn have a sincere passion for entrepreneurship, business analysis / consulting / development, and leadership development.

Social Media

Twitter: http://twitter.com/RealConquerLife

Facebook: http://facebook.com/TheConquerLifeMindset

To have Trey & Autumn speak to your organization or school, or for personal coaching please send inquiries to:

Conquerors@ConquerLifeMindset.com

You may also submit your inquiry online at:
http://www.ConquerLifeMindset.com

90392322R00069

Made in the USA
San Bernardino, CA
17 October 2018